GW00720717

THE AUDIO-WORKBOOK

The Instructional Design Library

Volume 5

THE AUDIO-WORKBOOK

Danny G. Langdon
Director of Instructional Design Research
The American College
Bryn Mawr, Pennsylvania

Danny G. Langdon
Series Editor

Educational Technology Publications
Englewood Cliffs, New Jersey 07632

Library of Congress Cataloging in Publication Data

Langdon, Danny G
    The audio-workbook.

    (The Instructional design library; v. no. 5)
    Bibliography: p.
    1. Audio-visual education. I. Title. II. Series.
LB1043.L28   371.33'3   77-25109
ISBN 0-87778-109-5

Printed in the United States of America.

Library of Congress Catalog Card Number: 77-25109.

International Standard Book Number: 0-87778-109-5.

First Printing: February, 1978.

PREFACE

Working in audio instruction continues to be a real challenge. If working in written instruction is like dealing with butter that is on the verge of melting, then working to make audio more effective is like trying to remain still while sitting on Jello. There is so much promise for audio and we have only begun to tap the benefits.

I personally suspect that our problem in audio instruction is that we often employ it at the wrong times and fail to make use of its simplicity. I've therefore tried to make the development of it simple and to match such development with what audio turns out to be—that is, audio and not written material that *sounds like written material* but not audio. I have only begun to explore all of the techniques that enhance the effectiveness of audio instruction.

I owe much to The American College for giving me the opportunity to begin my first assignment for it in the audio medium. I believe we have demonstrated that this was just a beginning.

Danny G. Langdon

CONTENTS

ABSTRACT

THE AUDIO-WORKBOOK

There are a number of format layouts within which the workbook portion of the Audio-Workbook can be structured. In this book the reader is introduced to three such layouts. Of particular interest is the manner in which the unique features of audio are employed to enhance learning effectiveness. Directions are given in regard to what the design is, how it is used, and how to produce it in such a way as to assure that what is produced is audio—and not written instruction that sounds like written words.

The selection of audio as a delivery system for guiding student learning is not a whimsical matter. This book outlines certain justifications for the use of audio, mainly in terms of the needs to be found in an analysis of learner objectives, the facilitating function of audio, and administrative justifications. The reader will learn and see specific design formats that have been used, in meeting these justifications.

Finally, although not a specific aspect of an audio instructional design, a highly inexpensive, easy-to-use system is described which allows students to easily and quickly access any specific information on an audio-tape. This system, called Zimdex, was developed by the author and is illustrated within two of the instructional formats suggested for audio instruction.

THE AUDIO-WORKBOOK

I.

USE

With the current wide availability of cassette recorder/
playback units, instructional designs involving the audio-
tape medium are no longer exotic and out of financial reach
to teachers and students. Some might believe that a recording
studio and large associated expenses are still necessary to
produce and utilize audio, but such is not the case. *Home*
developed and produced recordings, with nothing more than
simple cassette recorder/player units, can provide students
with effective audio instruction when and where needed.
Instructional designs utilizing the audio medium have many
uses that do not require the high degree of professionalism
usually sought. There are instances in which nonprofessional
voice recording, music, and background effects, for instance,
are best for communicating at a level which makes students
feel most comfortable.

In this book you will be learning about one specific audio
instructional design, the Audio-Workbook; and, in particular,
a detailed procedure for producing the audio portion of the
instructional design. The general lack of clear and substantive
procedural guides given elsewhere to the development of the
audio medium justifies the inclusion of a detailed discussion
of a procedure for the development of this instructional
design. The Developmental Guide section of this book will
present an example of a project undertaken by the author

which illustrates how to *produce* audio instruction effectively and efficiently. The emphasis here will be on the use of audio for instructional purposes, rather than for purely informational transmission or the guidance of instructional events. In other words, the audio will present the content and the necessary interactive instruction for assuring that the content is learned.

Part of the "beauty" of audio is the ease with which the listener can stop and replay the message, much the same way as one can with the written medium (books). This fact offers interesting possibilities for presenting and controlling interaction requirements between the medium of audio, the listener, and an accompanying workbook. The listener need not simply listen, but can stop and answer questions, and receive feedback from either a written source or the audio-tape itself. However, the audio medium has apparent disadvantages. For instance, one cannot easily *skim* over the content, although the advent of so-called *compressed speech* is at least a helpful aid in this direction. Also, there is some difficulty in readily *reviewing* a specific segment of what one has listened to. However, even these two disadvantages are overcome by the use of the Zimdex system—an audio indexing system that has been developed in response to the need to easily and quickly access specific information anywhere on an audio-tape.

By far the most widely utilized *use* of audio instruction is for independent self-study. Audio cassettes, in particular, are increasingly finding their way into training and education, both at home and in *listening areas* within classrooms and libraries. This existing use of the audio medium is not itself the primary justification for independent study. Rather, it is the simple fact that the hardware most commonly used, the cassette player, is designed for *individual use*. Also, since the student may wish to replay a tape, in the same sense that he or she re-reads a segment of a book, it makes sense to provide audio instruction for the individual to use as he or she would prefer. For self-paced, individualized instruction, individual use would, of course, be paramount.

Valid justifications for the use of the audio medium are based on any one of three possible needs.

The first application is for learning or demonstrating learner *objectives* that absolutely *need* an audio medium. This use is based on the requirement implied by an analysis of the objectives we have defined for students to learn. For instance, if an objective called for the student to listen to a piece of music and to identify certain notes or style, audio is obviously required. This would be an instance in which the *conditions* of the objective required audio. Here is another example:

> The objective states: "Given a five minute class lecture, write a set of notes that distinguish the *Main Idea* from the *Supplementary Material*."

In order to perform and learn this objective, audio would be required, unless it were possible to provide a live teacher demonstration when and where needed. Since the latter would be difficult to control on an individual student-need basis, the audio medium is more practical. This is true for initial learning, practice, and subsequent testing.

Some objectives need audio in order to perform the behavioral specification of the objective itself; for instance, in language training, or when the student is to role-play or give an oral presentation. Here is a specific example:

> The objective states: "To a given policy (insurance) program, recite a closing interview, demonstrating at least six of the eight criteria outlined in this course."

In the objective above, it is the behavior itself (reciting a closing interview) that requires audio. This could, of course, be done in front of a teacher, but if audio is being used for self-study and the student must, in his initial learning, self-evaluate his or her own performance (say, against a check-list of key points and/or a representative example), then audio will provide a convenient means of presenting examples of *proper closing* and for the student to demonstrate to himself that he can give a closing presentation.

Objectives normally have three parts to them:

Conditions—that which will be given or must be present to elicit the performance.

Behavioral terms—the action verb linked to the content or skill.

Standards—the degree of accuracy to which the performance must be exercised.

As is often the case, conditions and standards may be implied, rather than stated in the objective statement itself. The behavioral terms will always be specified. Whether specified or implied, an analysis of an objective or set of objectives is a good starting point for determining when audio instruction is needed.

The second major application of audio is where audio can play a major role in *facilitating* learning. This refers to those learning situations in which the student must attend to more than one *slice* of information at a given time. For instance, when a student is reading detailed information relating to a chart, graph, or table of data, with various items physically separated from one another, he or she cannot look at the chart, graph, or table and also read the accompanying explanatory information. Typically, the student finds himself or herself reading a little, then holding a place in the book, and then glancing at the data-filled chart, and back to the reading. You will be doing this in this book, when instructions are given to look at an illustration, while information is being read. Worse yet, the problem is compounded by putting the chart or illustration on *another* page, which is often necessary. If, on the other hand, the student can *listen* to the information *and* look at the chart, he or she can then attend to both functions. This is what is meant by audio being used to *facilitate* learning.

The need for audio to *facilitate* learning is often also indicated by the objectives written for a course of study. Take the following objective, for example:

> The objective states: "Using the 1958 CSO Table, calculate the probability that an individual of a given age will die in a given year."

This objective, unlike the two previous objectives, does not indicate directly the need for audio because of *behavioral terms* or conditions. However, there are two parts of this objective which do indicate the *facilitating* function of audio. First is the *given* part of the objective, calling for the use of a table of information. Second is the indication that a *calculation* is to be performed. Audio is useful in guiding students through complicated mathematical formulas and related calculations. For this objective, audio instruction could be used to guide the student through the chart and to present information about the chart *while* the student is looking at it. Audio would also be useful, as explained, in guiding the student through formulas and equations he would have to employ in making necessary calculations. Hence, audio *facilitates* learning in this instance.

The third major application and justification for audio, and the one that often is used, and sometimes gets us into trouble, is administrative. Administrative needs include ease of distribution, a change of pace, efficiency, multi-uses (such as first in learning and then in subsequent use with potential clients), a desire to compress time (such as for a review), and similar instances. One should make *really* sure that audio is truly justified. Administrative justifications for the use of audio are not as valid in general as, say, uses based on the needs of objectives and for facilitating learning. However, we should not condemn administrative justifications. Sometimes they are real and necessary. Where one may be treading in deep waters is when audio is seen, like any medium or instructional strategy, as a *panacea* for solving all instructional problems.

For whatever reason audio is chosen, the Audio-Workbook instructional design will not change in its basic requirements.

II.

OPERATIONAL DESCRIPTION

If you have taken the opportunity to review any of the other instructional designs which comprise the *Instructional Design Library*, then you may find the following Operational Description to be one of the shortest in the series. The operational mechanics of an Audio-Workbook are simple, although varying levels of sophistication can be added in terms of what actually goes into the accompanying workbook, how and what the audio will be (music, non-music, single or multiple-voices, etc.), developmental procedures, or in terms of the audio hardware itself. We concentrate here, for example, on the use of a simple cassette playback unit. One is cautioned at this point not to let higher levels of sophistication prevent the use of this design, for the average producer and user will find effective instruction with the *basics* of audio instruction.

The reason this design is called Audio-Workbook, rather than an Audio, is that student interaction is a basic requirement. Interaction is necessary for achieving higher levels of learning effectiveness and efficiency (as with any instructional design). The principal need is to provide an opportunity for the student to demonstrate to himself or herself whether or not he or she is learning.

By interaction, we mean that the student should be more than a passive listener (as in the case of audio) or readerviewer (as in the case of written or visual media). Interaction, meaning specifically the opportunity for a student to respond to what he or she is learning, mainly through writing answers to questions, *and* receiving feedback (through answers to the questions), is necessary so that the student can judge whether learning is taking place. Of course, there are other forms of interaction, in which one manipulates, gives an oral presentation, and so forth. In the Audio-Workbook we will find the interaction to involve answering questions and receiving answers. This will mean actually taking the time to write out answers—not just mentally thinking through the answers.

The workbook is also to be employed, after its initial use for interaction, as a convenient source for subsequent review by students. As was pointed out early in the Use section, audio cannot be easily *skimmed* for review. The workbook, being a written component, can be reviewed. There are few students who would not like to have a record of their initial learning for review prior to the final achievement or criterion testing that is usually required.

The addition of a workbook to audio does place some limitations on where an audio instructional program can be used. For instance, professionals in business have increasingly made use of audio instruction in their automobiles while traveling to and from work or between seeing clients. One can hardly listen and also respond in a workbook while driving. If this is where audio instruction is to be used, other considerations are in order for maintaining interest, and vicarious interaction might be built into the audio instruction itself. In the far greater and common use of audio instruction, it is anticipated that the workbook part of the design could, would, and should be used.

In the workbook, it is possible to include, of course, certain visual aids that would help to support or be an integral aspect of the learning objectives. The examples to be used in this book will not, in general, include visual aids (other than graphs and tables), but it is obvious that they could be included. It is hoped that visuals would be used as they are really needed, rather than to add nothing more than attractive dressing to the program.

Operationally, the Audio-Workbook design is used by a student in the following manner:

1. Usually, the student is directed to a set of written behavioral objectives. This may be done after a brief overview introduction. In any case, it is usually before any detailed instruction is given via the audio. The objectives could be presented via the audio-tape, but printed objectives allow the student to take plenty of time to firmly *read* and store in his or her memory what he or she is to listen to and learn about. The usual one-time run-by of the audio-tape is insufficient for statements of objectives, particularly when there are several objectives to be stated at the beginning. The instructional developer is left with the option of stating the objectives as a printed list or in paragraph form.

2. Having read the objectives, the student is then directed to turn on the tape recorder and listen to the audio-tape. A presentation of content is given. Content is used here in the broad sense to include illustrations that appear in the workbook (i.e., graphs, visuals, etc.).

3. At appropriate points in the presentation of content, directions are given to answer questions related to the objective to be presented. Such questions are usually of two types: (1) those that aid the student in arriving at satisfactory performance of the objective (these we call *enabling* questions) and (2) questions which demand performance of the objective as stated (this type of question is commonly labeled a *criterion* or *terminal* question). Directions on the audio-tape can be given to answer a question printed in the

workbook, or the question itself may be given on the tape, with the response to be written in the workbook. Later, in the Design Format section of this book, some guidelines will be given as to where questions should appear.

4. Confirmations, or representative correct answers, to the student's written answer in the workbook, are then given. Confirmations may be printed in the workbook or given on the tape. Again, guidelines will be given later, in the Design Format section of this book.

5. The student is then given direction to continue the audio presentation for additional content, questions, confirmation, or to proceed to a new objective.

The preceding Operational Description has presented the audio-workbook as something which the student would use in a linear fashion. That is, he or she begins at the beginning of the audio-tape and proceeds to the end. This need not necessarily be so. Through use of the audio indexing system called Zimdex, the student may proceed to *any* given section within the audio-tape. This feature is particularly beneficial when a student needs to review or skip over instruction on objectives that have been learned previously. It also has some use where a *branching* format of instruction, similar to programmed instruction, is desired. Zimdex is described later in this book.

III.

DESIGN FORMAT

The design format of an Audio-Workbook consists of two basic components:

The Audio-Tape and
The Workbook.

Three audio-workbook programs will be used to illustrate this design.

The Audio-Tape

Describing the audio-tape is a difficult task. One would normally do so in terms of the *script* from which the tape is produced. The author is no less forced to do so, although, as will be described later, *there may be no written script produced*, such as the one shown in Figure 1.

The script you see illustrated in Figure 1 is rather straight-forward. Typically, writers add a second column for indicating where cues, music, etc., should occur in conjunction with what is read by a narrator. There are at least four things in particular to note about this script:

1. In paragraphs one and two, an overview approach is used to let the student know in general what is ahead of him on the tape. This also includes *affective* objectives to be achieved and the purpose or significance of instruction to the student.

2. In the third paragraph, directions are given to read

Figure 1

Sample Audio Script

This is the beginning of the review of Assignment 2, covering the topics of the Income Statement as well as Accounting Records and Systems. In discussing the Income Statement we will explain the accrual concept or the mating of revenues and expenses. The function of accounting records will be described as well as the effect of Adjusting and Closing Entries. Finally, the objectives of a properly designed accounting system will be reviewed.

The purpose of this review is to stress the importance of the Income Statement and the accounting processes which produce it. A second purpose is to identify and explain problems that arise in constructing and analyzing the Income Statement. A knowledge of accounting records and systems is essential to understanding the strengths and weaknesses of the Income Statement. The use to which this may be applied by you in Business Insurance in particular should be obvious enough, in that careful analysis of Income Statements is paramount to successful planning of insurance needs.

At the tone, stop the tape and turn to Page 2.1 in your response booklet. Read the objectives for Assignment 2; then restart the tape.

(tone)

Let's turn our attention first to some concepts that are related to income measurement. Two important concepts are the accrual concept and the mating concept. The accrual concept requires that periodic business income for a firm be measured by accounting for operating transactions which affect owners' equity. Revenue and expense transactions are those which either increase or decrease owners' equity as a result of normal operations. It is important to understand that revenue and expense recognition, under the accrual concept, is not necessarily the same as accounting for cash flows.

For example, revenue transactions increase owners' equity and, for most business activities, involve an increase in accounts receivable, not cash, when the revenue transaction takes place. This happens because most American business is conducted on a credit basis, not a cash basis.

Suppose, for example, that a sale is made on account in 1971 and that the cash is collected from the customer in 1972. The accrual

(Continued on next page)

Figure 1 (Continued)

concept requires that the revenue be properly recognized in 1971 because it is the sale on account, not the ultimate collection of cash, which affects the owners' equity. Suppose that the salesman's commission on this sale is paid to him in 1972. The accrual concept requires that the commission expense be recognized in 1971, the year in which owners' equity was reduced by this operating transaction, and not in 1972, the year in which the payment was made to the salesman.

The accrual concept is closely identified with the matching concept. The matching concept requires that Income Statements show revenues for the given accounting period and the expenses which are properly associated with or matched against those revenues.

Thus, the accrual concept deals with the proper recognition and measurement of revenues and expenses for an accounting period. The matching process deals with the proper association or matching of expenses against revenues for the period. Hence, the accrual concept is often described as the matching concept.

Now, answer Question One on Page 2.2 of your response booklet.

(tone)

Another concept that is related to income measurement is the cost concept. What is the relationship between the cost concept and expense? The cost concept tells us that an asset is usually recorded at the acquisition price. That is, the original historical cost incurred to acquire it.

How is this cost concept related to expense? An expense is that portion of the cost of the asset that has expired. We usually recognize and measure the cost expiration on the basis of a decline in the utility or usefulness of the asset. Therefore, when we recognize cost expiration, part of the acquisition price, the original cost of the asset becomes an expired cost or, in other words, an expense.

At the tone, turn to Page 2.4 of your response booklet and answer the following question. (Pause) Question Two is: *What is the relationship between the cost concept and expense?*

(tone)

Your answer to Question Two should reflect that the cost concept states that an asset is ordinarily recorded at the acquisition price, that

(Continued on next page)

Figure 1 (Continued)

is, the original cost incurred to acquire it. On the other hand, an expense is an expired cost. The recognition or measurement of cost expiration is based upon the decline in the usefulness of the asset. Therefore, the amount at which the asset is originally recorded, that is, the cost or acquisition price, becomes an expense upon expiration.

Now, let's continue our discussion with a review of the calculation of gross profit. Gross profit or gross margin is a very important benchmark figure to which businessmen refer in trying to evaluate the results of business operations.

Suppose you were given a list of Balance Sheet and Income Statement items, that is, accounts and dollar balances. Would you be able to pick out the items and the dollar amounts and set them up in such a way as to compute the gross margin or gross profit? You should remember that gross profit or gross margin is the arithmetic (ar-ith-MET-ic) difference between net sales and the merchandise cost of goods sold.

The first step in the calculation of gross margin is to compute the net sales. Net sales is found by subtracting both sales returns and allowances and sales discounts from gross sales. Note that there are two items which must be subtracted from gross sales to arrive at net sales.

Next, the merchandise cost of goods sold is subtracted from net sales to obtain the gross profit figure. Once the gross profit has been obtained, the other operating expenses—selling expenses and administrative expenses—can be subtracted from that amount to determine the net income figure.

Now, answer question three of Page 2.6 in your response booklet.

(tone)

the objectives printed in the workbook. If the audio instruction is concerned with only one or two objectives, they might be given on the audio-tape, although it is still wise to include them in the workbook also.

3. Following a content presentation, directions are given to answer questions on specific pages of the workbook; or the question, depending largely on its length and complexity, might be asked on the tape itself. In the illustration, the first question is given in the workbook, and the second one is given on the audio-tape.

4. There is an indication made of where a tone should be given as a signal for the student to stop the tape, when necessary, and answer the question(s).

The Workbook

Concentrating on the format the workbook might take, rather than on the audio-tape at this point in the description of the Audio-Workbook, affords several advantages. First, it provides a convenient way to point out the direction the script itself must take. That is, like almost any instructional design, it is the objectives and necessary interaction (usually questions and answers, and visual needs such as graphs, tables, etc.) which must be defined initially and toward which the audio will be directed. Second, it affords a convenient way to introduce certain innovations which enhance the effectiveness and utility of an audio approach to learning—for instance, the use of the Zimdex system.

The workbook can take several different forms, three of which are illustrated below. These are labeled the Cassette/Review Program, the Mathematics Program, and the Update Program.

The Cassette/Review Program Workbook

This particular program is representative of the use of audio for straightforward content presentation. It is for instructional/learning purposes, rather than simply information transmission. In this instance, the intent was for instructional review of a semester-length finance and accounting course. The workbook is illustrated in Figures 2.1-2.5. The script previously illustrated, in Figure 1, is related to these sample workbook pages.

You will recall from the previous description of the audiotape that the Audio-Workbook program begins on the tape (rather than from within the workbook) by a brief overview. The first part of Figure 1 illustrates the opening statement. At the end of this statement, the student is directed to a set of objectives to read. These objectives are illustrated in Figure 2.1. By listening to the overview and reading the objectives, the student should have a clear understanding of where the audio presentation will be heading. A simple direction, *Turn on the Tape*, at the bottom of the objectives page tells the student to begin the audio presentation again. Thus, in this example, the script information would be heard following the first tone in Figure 1.

The need for clear direction, such as an overview and list of specific objectives to be attained by the student, is probably more important in audio instruction than in any other medium. Audio instruction presents special problems. In the written medium, the student can easily re-read and *skim* ahead. Generally, in visual instruction our attention is sustained. However, in audio instruction there is more likelihood of our *drifting* away from what is being said, let alone what is coming next. An overview and explicit set of directions as to what to anticipate happening is more likely to keep the listener attentive. It is important, as well, that the objectives be of a number and level of complexity that can be easily remembered. The *list* of objectives must not be too long nor detailed. It is a good idea, half way through the program, to remind the student to re-read the list of objectives. This might also be accomplished by a review of the objectives on the tape itself.

Assuming that the listener has *listened* to the overview and *read* the objectives, and *listened* to a content presentation, the next requirement is the provision for the student to demonstrate learning of the objectives. Figure 2.2 illustrates a question page. You may recall from the audio-script example that the student was referred to this question by the audio-tape. Question 2, on the other hand, is given on the tape itself, and the student is referred to answer the question in the workbook (see Figure 2.3). The listener is always encouraged to write his answers out and never to just *mentally* think the answer through. The main reason for placing some questions *on the tape* and others in the workbook is to keep the listener alert. When all the questions (and answers) are solely in the workbook, there is a tendency to listen a little less to the audio presentation. Realizing that there is a mixture of questions on and off the tape keeps the listener alert.

Figures 2.2, 2.4, and 2.5 illustrate questions that are printed in the workbook. The question in Figure 2.2 could have been given on the tape in that it is relatively brief and could be easily *remembered* by the listener. Usually, brief questions, such as the one which was asked for question 2, can be given on the tape. Figure 2.4, however, is a question with several facts and figures which the listener could not possibly remember if conveyed via the tape, therefore it must be printed in the workbook. This is usually the case when calculations of mathematics problems are involved. Figure 2.5 illustrates a multiple-choice question, and such questions always must be printed in the workbook. In all instances, immediately following the space in which the student writes

(discussion continues on Page 25)

Figure 2.1

HS 305
ASSIGNMENT 2

When you have completed the Review of Assignment 2, you will:

1. Explain why the accrual concept is often described as the matching concept.

2. Explain the relationship between the cost concept and expense.

3. Given a sample problem of accounts and balances, compute the gross profit or gross margin.

4. Describe the ultimate effect of the adjusting process on account balances, and the purpose of the adjusting process.

5. Describe the ultimate effect of the closing process on balances of both nominal and real accounts, and the purpose of the closing process.

6. List the four major objectives which a properly designed accounting system should achieve.

7. Given possible statements concerning the accounting process, identify the correct statements.

Turn on the tape.

Page A*

---

*Note to Reader: In reality page numbers are used here rather than letters. Letters are used here only to avoid confusion with page numbers in this book.

Figure 2.2

HS 305
ASSIGNMENT 2

Question 1

Explain why the accrual concept is often described as the matching concept.

Check your answer on Page C

Answer to Question 1

The accrual concept deals with the proper recognition and measurement of revenues and expenses for an accounting period, and the matching process deals with the proper association or matching of expenses against revenues for the period. Hence, the accrual concept is often described as the matching concept.

Turn on the tape.

Figure 2.3

HS 305
ASSIGNMENT 2

Question 2

(When you hear the tone, write your answer below.)

The answer is given on the tape.

Turn on the tape.

Page D

Page E

Figure 2.4

HS 305
ASSIGNMENT 2

Question 3

Using the following accounts and balances, computer the gross profit or gross margin:

Gross sales	$150,000.
Sales returns and allowances	13,000.
Sales discounts	2,000.
Merchandise cost of goods sold	85,000.
Selling and general expenses	40,000.

Check your answer on Page G

Page F

Answer to Question 3

$50,000 ... computed as follows:

Gross sales		$150,000.
Less: Sales returns and allowances	$13,000.	
Sales discounts	2,000.	
Net sales		$135,000.
Less: Merchandise cost of goods sold		85,000.
Gross profit or gross margin		$50,000.

Turn on the tape.

Page G

Figure 2.5

HS 305
ASSIGNMENT 2

Question 7

Check the line beside the numbers for the correct statements concerning the accounting process.

I.   The most important part of the accounting process is the analysis of transactions because this requires determining which accounts should be debited or credited and the amounts involved.

II.   Journalizing is the procedure of recording transactions in subsidiary ledger accounts.

III.   Posting is the mechanical step of recording changes in ledger accounts as specified by journal entries.

IV.   The adjusting process involves transferring balances from all nominal accounts to the profit and loss summary account.

V.   The preparation of financial statements requires judgment as to arrangement and terminology.

            ...... A.   I and II only.
            ...... B.   III and IV only.
            ...... C.   I and IV only.
            ...... D.   I, III, and V only.
            ...... E.   II, IV, and V only.

The answer is given on the tape.

Turn on the tape.   Page N

his or her answer, directions are given as to where the representative, correct answer to the question is to be found. This brings us to a description of the third part of the workbook—the answers.

The confirming answers, which provide the student with feedback on the correctness of his or her responses, like the questions themselves, may be printed in the workbook or given on the tape. *Where* the answers appear depends on the length and complexity of the answers. In Figure 2.2 the answer is given in the workbook (below, or across on the next page, or on the reverse side of the question page). If the answer is in the workbook, it is suggested that the answer appear directly opposite the page on which the question is asked. This allows a convenient comparison. There is much debate on whether the answer should be *hidden*, but convenience to the student should take preference; simply place the burden on the student not to *cheat* the system. If a student really wants to *cheat*, he or she *will*, no matter what is done.

In Figure 2.3, the answer is given on the tape. It is a relatively brief answer; and while the student is hearing it, he or she can easily compare this to the written answer.

In Figure 2.4, the answer is printed in the workbook. This answer involves details, and there is a need to see the comparison between the student's written answer and the correct answer.

In Figure 2.5, the answer is given on the tape. This is usually the case with multiple-choice type questions. This is partly because a simple letter answer is given, but also because the listener can be directed to what is wrong, if necessary, with the other statements. The listener can look and listen, in this case, at the same time.

Of course, there is no answer page when an answer is given on the tape. In such instances, directions should be given at the bottom of the question page to *Turn on the Tape*. Such directions, including when the lesson is finished, may sound like obvious points. However, when you have an audio-tape running or stopped, it is necessary to know *exactly where to go next*.

Finally, a workbook is not restricted to objectives, questions, and answers. Charts and visuals may be included. Some of this will be illustrated in the next example. This workbook has emphasized simplicity. Many degrees of sophistication can be added.

The Mathematics Program Workbook

The second workbook example to be illustrated features some additional ways in which the workbook can be structured. The primary justification for use of audio in this instance is that audio *facilitates* learning. You will recall that this use was primarily for instances in which charts, graphs, mathematical calculations, and such were to be learned, and that a dual demand would be placed on the student's attention, i.e., looking at a graph and listening. In the following illustration there are both mathematical calculations and tables of information to be studied. A mathematics program from an introductory insurance course is illustrated in Figures 3.1 through 3.8. Your attention is focused first on the workbook design and then on the use of audio instruction.

Peruse the design layout in Figures 3.1 through 3.4. You will observe a unit of instruction based on a specific learner objective, composed of five basic components: objective, example, instruction, questions, and answers.

The objective, Figure 3.1, is the target of student learning and the first point of entry into the instructional unit. This is followed by an example—a question. The example is completed, if possible, by the student to gain some initial assessment of his or her understanding (mastery) of the objective before proceeding, if necessary, to specific instruction. If the student is able to correctly work the example (the correct answer to which is found on the answer sheet, Figure 3.4), then he or she simply bypasses the instruction segment and proceeds to try the question section (Figure 3.3). If the question segment can be satisfactorily completed, then the student goes on to the next unit, which is a new objective (Figure 3.6). If, on the other hand, the student is unable to complete either the example or question segments correctly, then he or she is told to complete the instruction segment (beginning in Figure 3.1). This flow of learning may be illustrated by the following diagram:

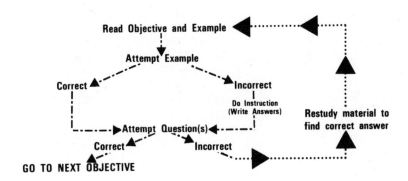

You can see that this workbook format features a bypass function so as to account for any possible knowledge the student already possesses on certain, and possibly all, objectives. We now focus our attention on where the audio component is used.

In the instruction segment, Figures 3.1 through 3.2, written instruction and audio instruction are illustrated. It was judged in this particular objective that written instruction would suffice for some of the objective and that audio was

(discussion continues on Page 36)

Figure 3.1

Objective 09.10   Demonstrate familiarity with the structure of the
                         1958 Commissioner's Standard Ordinary Table by
                         filling in data given in a partially completed sec-
                         tion of the table to complete that section.

Example 09.10   The following is a portion of the 1958 Commis-
                         sioner's Standard Ordinary Table. How many per-
                         sons will be living at the beginning of the 51st
                         year?

| | *Number Living at Beginning of* | *Number Dying During* |
Age	*Designated Year*	*Designated Year*
50	8,762,306	72,902
51	—————	79,160
52	8,610,244	85,758
53	8,524,486	92,832
54	8,431,654	100,337

Instruction   Read LIFE INSURANCE
                             Huebner & Black
                             Pages 324-329

1. What does the mortality rate represent?

2. Define the term *radix*.

Figure 3.2

3. For this portion of the instruction, you will need (a) the 1958 CSO Mortality Table on pages 325 and 326 of your textbook, and (b) a cassette recorder. After you have assembled these materials, turn on the tape—Zimdex #1.

4. Using the table below calculate:

   (a) the mortality rate at age 1.
   (b) the mortality rate at age 2.
   (c) the mortality rate at age 3.

Age	Deaths	Number Exposed to Death
1	60	10,000
2	120	30,000
3	240	80,000

Figure 3.3

Question   Using the portion of the 1958 Commissioner's Standard
            Ordinary Table shown below, calculate:

            (a) number living at age 10.
            (b) number dying at age 4.
            (c) mortality rate per 1,000 at age 0.

            Write your answers in the blocks provided.

Age	Number Living at Beginning of Designated Year (l_x)	Number Dying During Designated Year (d_x)	Yearly Probability of Dying (q_x)	Yearly Probability of Surviving (p_x)
0	10,000,000	70,800	(c)	.99292
1	9,929,200	17,475	.00176	.99824
2	9,911,725	15,066	.00152	.99848
3	9,896,659	14,449	.00146	.99854
4	9,882,210	(b)	.00140	.99860
5	9,868,375	13,322	.00135	.99865
6	9,855,053	12,812	.00130	.99870
7	9,842,241	12,401	.00126	.99874
8	9,829,840	12,091	.00123	.99877
9	9,817,749	11,879	.00121	.99879
10	(a)	11,865	.00121	.99879
11	9,794,005	12,047	.00123	.99877
12	9,781,958	12,325	.00126	.99874
13	9,769,633	12,896	.00132	.99868
14	9,756,737	13,562	.00139	.99861
15	9,743,175	14,225	.00146	.99854
16	9,728,950	14,983	.00154	.99846
17	9,713,967	15,737	.00162	.99838
18	9,698,230	16,390	.00169	.99831
19	9,681,840	16,846	.00174	.99826
20	9,664,994	17,300	.00179	.99821
21	9,647,694	17,655	.00183	.99817
22	9,630,039	17,912	.00186	.99814
23	9,612,127	18,167	.00189	.99811
24	9,593,960	18,324	.00191	.99809
25	9,575,636	18,481	.00193	.99807
26	9,557,155	18,732	.00196	.99804
27	9,538,423	18,981	.00199	.99801
28	9,519,442	19,324	.00203	.99797
29	9,500,118	19,760	.00208	.99792
30	9,480,358	20,193	.00213	.99787
31	9,460,165	20,718	.00219	.99781
32	9,439,447	21,239	.00225	.99775
33	9,418,208	21,850	.00232	.99768
34	9,396,358	22,551	.00240	.99760
35	9,373,807	23,528	.00251	.99749

Figure 3.4

Answer Sheet

Example 09.10   The answer is: 8,689,404

Instruction   The answers are:

           4. (a) .006
              (b) .004
              (c) .003

Question   The answers are:

        (a) 9,805,870
        (b) 13,835
        (c) .00708

Figure 3.5

			Amount of 1 Due Per Year	Present Value of 1 Due Per Year
		TABLE I		
		SELECTED COMPOUND INTEREST FUNCTIONS		
		(4½ percent interest)		
Years	Amount of 1	Present Value of 1		
1	$(1.045)^1 = 1.045000$	$(1/1.045)^1 = .956938$	1.045000	1.000000
2	$(1.045)^2 = 1.092025$	$(1/1.045)^2 = .915730$	2.137025	1.956938
3	$(1.045)^3 = 1.141166$	$(1/1.045)^3 = .876297$	3.278191	2.872668
4	$(1.045)^4 = 1.192519$	$(1/1.045)^4 = .838561$	4.470710	3.748964
5	$(1.045)^5 = 1.246182$	$(1/1.045)^5 = .802451$	5.716892	4.587526
6	$(1.045)^6 = 1.302260$	$(1/1.045)^6 = .767896$	7.019152	5.389977
7	$(1.045)^7 = 1.360862$	$(1/1.045)^7 = .734828$	8.380014	6.157872
8	$(1.045)^8 = 1.422101$	$(1/1.045)^8 = .703185$	9.802114	6.892701
9	$(1.045)^9 = 1.486095$	$(1/1.045)^9 = .672904$	11.288209	7.595886
10	$(1.045)^{10} = 1.552969$	$(1/1.045)^{10} = .643928$	12.841179	8.268790
11	$(1.045)^{11} = 1.622853$	$(1/1.045)^{11} = .616199$	14.464032	8.912718
12	$(1.045)^{12} = 1.695881$	$(1/1.045)^{12} = .589664$	16.159913	9.528917
13	$(1.045)^{13} = 1.772196$	$(1/1.045)^{13} = .564272$	17.932109	10.118581
14	$(1.045)^{14} = 1.851945$	$(1/1.045)^{14} = .539973$	19.784054	10.682852
15	$(1.045)^{15} = 1.935282$	$(1/1.045)^{15} = .516720$	21.719337	11.222825

Figure 3.6

Objective 09.20   Use a table of compound interest functions to determine the value to which the amount of 1 will ac-
cumulate to in any given period of years.

Example 09.20   According to Table I, which of the following amounts
is the amount that 1 would accumulate to at the end
of 3 years?

...... A. 1.045000
...... B. 1.092025
...... C. 1.141166
...... D. 3.278191

Instruction   1. For this portion of the instruction, you will need
Table I and a cassette recorder. After you have
assembled these materials, turn on the tape—
Zimdex #52.

FIGURE 1

$1 + (1 \times .045) = 1 + .045 = 1.045$

FIGURE 2

$1.045 + (1.045 \times .045) = 1.045 + .047025 = 1.092025$

Figure 3.7

FIGURE 3

1.092025 + (1.092025 x .045) = 1.092025 + .049141125
= 1.141166

FIGURE 4

$(1.045)^3$ = 1.045 x 1.045 x 1.045 = 1.141166

2. According to Table I, what would the amount of 1 accumulate to in

(a)   4 years
(b)   6 years
(c) 12 years

Question   According to Table I, what would the amount of 1 accumulate to in

(a)   5 years
(b) 10 years
(c) 15 years

Figure 3.8

Answer Sheet

Example 09.20   The answer is: "C".

Instruction   The answers are:

   (a) 1.192519
   (b) 1.302260
   (c) 1.695881

Question   The answers are:

   (a) 1.246182
   (b) 1.552969
   (c) 1.935282

necessary for another part (where a table of information was to be used). Thus, in Figure 3.1 a text reference is given and questions asked. In Figure 3.2, a table—the 1958 C.S.O. Mortality Table—was referenced and an audio cassette is used. The audio instruction in this case guides the student through a detailed table (Figure 3.3) and explains the various columns of data and their relationship to one another. Again, the student answers a series of questions (Figure 3.2) and in this instance is guided by the audio-tape to do so. Upon completion of both the written and audio instruction, the student will then complete the questions which test the objective as a whole, in Figure 3.3. The answers to the example, the questions as part of the instruction, and the questions which test the objective are located in all cases on a separate sheet in the workbook, as seen in Figure 3.4.

Figures 3.5 through 3.8 illustrate the same basic design format of objective, example, instruction, questions, and answers, but your attention is directed to a use of audio instruction in a different way. You will note in the instruction segment (Figure 3.6) that audio is used as the only instructional source. Audio in this instance not only guides the student through a table of data (Figure 3.5), but also through a mathematical calculation. As the student listens to the tape, he or she is referred to illustrations of mathematical calculations within the Instruction segment, in Figures 3.6 and 3.7. Here, again, the student can be looking at the calculations while listening—a function that would be impossible if he or she had to read and look at calculations.

In concluding the Mathematics Program illustration, you have most likely noted the reference to Zimdex. Zimdex is discussed in some detail within the final illustration, which follows.

The Update Program Workbook

The Update Program is illustrated in Figures 4.1 through 4.6. Students who have completed courses in taxation use this program to update their information on practices studied in the past. This illustration will exhibit a slight variation in the workbook format and the means by which any specific audio portion may be easily accessed at any point on the tape.

The workbook is divided in this program into three major sections: (1) introduction, (2) objectives, and (3) questions-notes-answers.

The first section, Figure 4.1, contains an introductory *Purpose and Significance*—an overview of why this area of taxation is important and what it relates to in a generic sense. This is followed by a list of *Supplementary References* which the student may wish to use in addition to the instruction that is provided by the audio-tape. The audio-tape is meant to carry the instruction for the most part, but Supplementary References contain details on working examples and sources the student may also find of direct benefit. The cassettes which the student will need to use are listed at the bottom of the Introduction.

The second section, Figure 4.2, is a list of all the objectives related to the topic outlined in the *Purpose* and *Significance*. Since this is an *Update* program, it is presupposed that the student will not need to update himself or herself on every objective, but rather only on those which have not been used for some time. Students are directed to read the list of objectives and check off those on which they will update themselves. A specific page reference in the workbook follows each objective so that further directions can be given as to where the update is located on the audio cassette. Let us suppose, for example, that the student is going to update himself on Objective #1, workbook page 94. This

objective is illustrated in Figure 4.3, and continues in Figure
4.4.

In Figure 4.3 we see that the objective the student is
going to update is listed once more. This not only tells
the student that he or she is on the correct page, but sets
the target of learning. The supplementary reference that
relates to the objective is also listed. Space is provided
to take notes as the tape is heard, and this is followed by
questions (Figure 4.4) and confirming answers to the questions. The questions in this illustration are asked on the
tape, as illustrated in the Review Program. With this brief
overview of the workbook component in mind, attention
is directed to the audio portion of the program. In Figure 4.3, following the objective, note the following reference:

Audio/Cassette #4   Zimdex #211

All of the information in this program is contained on
audio-tape cassettes (with the exception of *Supplementary
References*). The problem presented in this illustration is that
the student will not necessarily use all of the cassettes (of
which there are eight in the total program) or any single
cassette in a *linear* fashion. If, for example, Cassette #4
contains information covering the following objectives:

   the previous unit objectives #37 and 38

   the present unit objectives #1, 2, 3, 4, 5, 6, and 7,

how does the student find on the cassette where the information begins for the objective he wants to listen to—in this
example, the information for objective #1? Remember, he
or she may not have *updated* himself or herself on objectives
#37 and #38, so the tape is not at the point of beginning
objective #1. Also, suppose this student were with a client
and wanted to access information on any of these objectives and play it for his client. This is not an unusual problem
in any audio program. How does one easily and quickly find

(discussion continues on Page 47)

Figure 4.1

Taxation of the Proprietorship and Its Proprietor

Purpose and Significance

The sole proprietorship is the most basic and simple type of business ownership wherein a single individual owns the enterprise and all of its assets. The business is customarily conducted by the owner, who is usually the manager, with the assistance of any agents or employees that he may hire.

Since there are thousands of sole proprietorships throughout the country and the growth of these businesses continues to be encouraged by the many advantages of this mode of business, it is important that the life underwriter has a working knowledge of some of the rules that apply specifically to the individual as a businessman operating a sole proprietorship. These would include the procedure for determining an individual's income tax liability, the various contribution and distribution aspects of H.R. 10 plans, and the federal tax consequences of an insured proprietorship buy-sell agreement.

Supplementary References You May Need

1. C.L.U. Course 4 Study Guide (73), Assignment 14; *Pension Planning: Profit Sharing and Other Deferred Compensation Plans* (rev. ed. 72), Melone & Allen.
2. C.L.U. Course 5 Study Guide (73), Assignments 1 and 2; *Stanley & Kilcullen's Income Tax Law* (5th ed.), Parker.
3. C.L.U. Course 9 Study Guide (73), Assignment 8; *Business Insurance* (3rd ed.), White.
4. IRS Publication #17, *Your Federal Income Tax, 1973 Edition*, Chapters 7, 9, and 15.

Audio/Cassettes Needed
Cassettes #4 and #5

(Continued on next page)

Figure 4.1 (Continued)

Proceed to Page 93 and read each Objective. Check off those on which you wish to update yourself, and then proceed to the appropriate page reference for each objective.

Figure 4.2

Taxation of the Proprietorship and Its Proprietor

<table>
<tr><td>*Objectives:*</td><td></td><td>*Page*</td></tr>
<tr><td>...... 1.</td><td>List the five-step procedure for determining an individual's income tax liability.</td><td>94</td></tr>
<tr><td>...... 2.</td><td>Explain the significance of the terms *income averaging, minimum tax on preference items,* and *maximum tax on earned income.*</td><td>96</td></tr>
<tr><td>...... 3.</td><td>Define the following four terms used in the Self-Employed Individual's Tax Retirement Act (H.R. 10); (1) owner-employee, (2) self-employed individual, (3) full-time employee, and (4) regular (common law) employee.</td><td>98</td></tr>
<tr><td>...... 4.</td><td>Describe the limitations placed on contributions for owner-employees under H.R. 10 plans, and explain the vesting provisions prequired where an owner-employee participates in an H.R. 10 plan.</td><td>100</td></tr>
</table>

. . . .

...... *Problem* 1. Compute the maximum deductible contribution an owner-employee may make on his own behalf given a hypothetical H.R. situation.   102

. . . .

<table>
<tr><td>...... 5.</td><td>Given a list of statements concerning the deductibility of contributions under an H.R. 10 plan, identify any statements which are correct.</td><td>104</td></tr>
<tr><td>...... 6.</td><td>Describe three general conditions under which distributions may be made from an H.R. 10 plan without restrictions or penalty to an owner-employee, and explain the penalties imposed if a premature distribution is made in violation of these restrictions.</td><td>106</td></tr>
</table>

(Continued on next page)

Figure 4.2 (Continued)

...... 7.   Describe the impact of federal income and estate tax-
          es on death benefits payable under H.R. 10 plans for
          (a) self-employed individuals, and (b) regular (com-
          mon law) employees.   108

...... 8.   Given a list of statements concerning federal tax con-
          sequences of an insured proprietorship buy-sell plan,
          identify any statement(s) which are correct.   110

Figure 4.3

Taxation of the Proprietorship and Its Proprietor

Objective 1: List the five-step procedure for determining an individual's income tax liability.

Primary Reference: *Audio/Cassette #4   Zimdex #211*
Supplementary Reference: C.L.U. Course 5, Assignment 1, and Stanley & Kilcullen's *Federal Income Tax Law*.

(Page 94)

. . . .

NOTES

Figure 4.4

QUESTION 1
    Write your answer below.

Check Your Answer Below.

. . . .

ANSWER The five steps in the determination of an individual's income tax liability are:

1. Determine gross income.
2. Determine adjusted gross income.
3. Determine taxable income.
4. Compute the tax.
5. Determine the amount of tax due (incolves subtracting any credits allowable).

Proceed to the Next Objective You Have Selected.

Figure 4.5

Taxation of the Proprietorship and Its Proprietor

Problem 1: Compute the maximum deductible contribution an owner-
employee may make on his own behalf given a hypothetical
H.R. 10 situation.
Note: Read Objective 4.

Primary Reference: *Audio/Cassette #4*   *Zimdex #416*
Note: The audio portion also covers
Objective 4.
Supplementary Reference: See Objective 3.

. . . .

NOTES

Figure 4.6

PROBLEM 1

Hardsole is the owner-operator of a shoe store. His earned income this year before contributions to a Self-Employed Individual's Tax Retirement Act (H.R. 10) plan was $24,000.

If Hardsole contributes $500 a year toward the H.R. 10 plan for his dissident (and only) employee whose earnings were $10,000, compute the maximum deductible contribution Hardsole may make on his own behalf.

Check Your Answer Below.

. . . .

ANSWER   The maximum amount Hardsole can contribute on his own account is $1,175. He must first reduce his $24,000 earned income by the contributions made on behalf of his employee. This lowers his earned income to $23,500 ($24,000 − $500 = (23,500).

The $500 contribution was 5% of his employee's salary of $10,000. Therefore, the maximum Hardsole can contribute on his own behalf is 5% of his earned income, $23,500. This figure is $1,175.

Proceed to the Next Objective You Have Selected.

specific information on an audio tape? The answer lies in the use of the Zimdex system.

Zimdex works like a table of contents and page numbers in a book. If you were told to turn to page 25 in this book, you would have no difficulty in doing so. The same is true with Zimdex. Zimdex works as follows.

On one side of an audio-tape cassette, let us say Side A, the audio information is recorded. In our illustration, this would include all the instructional information for objectives 37 and 38 of the previous unit and objectives 1 through 7 of the present unit. On Side B, however, is recorded a series of numbers beginning with one and on through, say, 600, with a five second pause (or tone) between each number. Now, once these two sides of the tape are recorded together, we can match the beginning of the information for each objective on Side A with the number on Side B. For example, our illustrative objectives have the following numbers:

Objective	ZIMDEX
37	1
38	157
1	211
2	250
3	384
4	416
5	447
6	481
7	503

Now, to find the beginning of audio information on objective #1, you would place your cassette on Side B—the Zimdex side—and fast-forward or reverse, and stop and listen until you hear the number 211. When you hear this number, you immediately stop the tape recorder, turn the cassette to Side A, and the audio information would begin. The same procedure would be followed to find any objective on the audio-tape. You are told what Zimdex number the objective is keyed to, and you find it on the audio-tape cassette, Side B, and then turn the tape to Side A and hear the information. This is Zimdex. Most students can readily find the beginning point of audio information in this manner within 30 seconds or less. A step-by-step explanation at the beginning of a program, with sample illustrations to practice, will generally suffice in explaining to students how to use the Zimdex system. Zimdex was developed by The American College, Bryn Mawr, Pa., and may be used by anyone, provided due credit is given The American College as follows:

    Zimdex: The Audio Indexing System of The American
              College, Bryn Mawr, Pennsylvania

You probably noticed from the list of objectives and Zimdex numbers that as the objective number increases (let us say, from objective 1 to 7), that the Zimdex numbers get larger (from 211 to 503). When one is listening to the Zimdex numbers on Side B, the numbers would be heard in a descending order (i.e., 211, 210, 209, 208, etc.). This is a minor point, but our natural reaction would be to stop and push or advance the forward lever on the recorder with the thought of taking us to a higher number. However, since the numbers are descending, this is not the case. One would have to press the reverse lever. It is suggested that the numbers be recorded on Side B in an ascending order, rather than the descending order illustrated here.

Now, to return to the explanation of the Update Program, you can see that after completing the first objective in Figures 4.3 and 4.4, the student might proceed to the objective in Figure 4.5, identifying the Zimdex number given (#416), and proceed to listen to the audio portion for that objective. In so doing, the student has easily and quickly bypassed the audio instruction on objectives 2, 3, and 4 listed in Figure 4.2—objectives the student has presupposed and, in this case, decided not to update himself on. Zimdex, in this sense, is one means of enhancing the utility of audio instruction.

Summary

It has been the author's intent in the Design Format section of this book to illustrate a variety of ways in which to structure the workbook of the Audio-Workbook design and the outline certain considerations related to the audio portion and how its utility can be enhanced.

The Cassette/Review Program illustrated a straightforward instructional approach with no frills, but plenty of interaction and feedback. The Mathematics Program illustrated the use of pretesting to allow bypass of instruction already known by the student and the integration of written instruction with audio instruction. Finally, the Update Program illustrated how audio instruction can be indexed to allow entry into the audio portion when and where needed.

In conclusion, the reader is reminded to take into account the part which *time* plays in audio instruction. We often hear or read that audio instruction should be in reasonably small dosages—not to exceed, in general, about 15 minutes at a setting. Of course, it depends on the student, the content material, and the audio niceties (music, humor, etc.) which are incorporated to sustain interest in listening. It is a practical and necessary matter that audio instruction should indeed be given in small amounts.

IV.

OUTCOMES

The Audio-Workbook will be efficient and effective in guiding student learning when, first, it is chosen for uses which justify its need, and second, if the student is provided with interactive components and corresponding feedback.

The Audio-Workbook is effective because it encompasses the use of interactive instruction. It provides the means for students to test their own mastery of what they have listened to. They are more than passive auditors. The primary outcome of this interaction should be more effective student learning. Interaction, of course, also assists the developer in the validation process, leading to higher levels of learning effectiveness.

It can also be anticipated that learning efficiency will be improved through the use of the Zimdex system of accessing audio instruction. Indexing tapes allows quick and easy access to what the student wants. It also makes the process of replay much easier to achieve, which in the past has often been listed as one of the disadvantages of audio.

Finally, it is the author's contention that audio instruction can be enhanced in its effectiveness if proper procedures are followed in the manner in which it is produced. This seems obvious enough, but it means more than merely trying to do a good job of writing, recording a script, and reproducing audio. In the same sense that we can be assured, generally speaking, that the addition of objectives and the providing of interaction will enhance learning effectiveness, the way in which audio instruction is developed may also have an effect on its ultimate effectiveness. Good, clear writing of written materials is important in making a printed program under-standable at the level of the students who will use it. The same is no less so with audio. The difference we must recog-nize, however, is that one is the written word and the other is the spoken word. In audio production we generally start with the written word—a script—although what we are going to end up with is the spoken word—the audio-tape. If there are differences in the written word and spoken word, then it might make more sense to begin the development of audio instruction in the spoken word. In the following section, the suggested Developmental Guide to producing an Audio-Workbook program, we shall see how this can be done. The outcome could be a more effective audio program.

V.

DEVELOPMENTAL GUIDE

Figure 5, the Developmental Guide to an Audio-Workbook, is a detailed procedure of steps to be followed in producing and validating an Audio-Workbook. This particular guide is one the author developed and used in producing the Cassette/Review Program discussed earlier.

Our assumption in this developmental procedure is that we are going to be producing eight audio instructional units. Each unit would be composed of a set of learner objectives, limited in scope to a time frame that would be reasonable for the student to sit down and learn in one sitting—say, no more than 15 to 20 minutes.

The first two steps in the Developmental Guide are organizational steps of assigning a project team and meeting to go over responsibilities and this very Developmental Guide itself. A project team would usually consist of subject matter experts (SME), programmers (writers), team coordinator, and support personnel, such as typists and audio production personnel. If you are all of these rolled into one, the procedure involved still applies.

Steps 3, 4, and 5 involve analysis and approval of the outcomes of student learning. These specifications usually include two necessary components—the learner objectives and the criterion (terminal) questions which will test these objectives and which can be used by students to test their own

Figure 5

Developmental Guide to Audio-Workbook

	UNIT 1	2	3	4	5	6	7	8
1. Project Team Assigned								
2. Content Conference								
3. Questions and Ans. Written—SME								
Reviewed and Edit—Coor.								
4. Objectives Written—Prog.								
Objectives Approved—SME								
5. Obj. and Questions Reviewed— Coor.								
6. Record Content—SME								
Transcribe Recording—Sec.								
7. Script Edited—SME								
8. Questions, cues, etc., added— Prog.								
9. Criterion Test Written—Prog.								
Criterion Test Approved—SME								
10. 1st Draft Program Review—Coor.								
11. Script Typed—Sec.								
Script Proofed—Sec.								
12. Workbook Typed—Sec.								
Workbook Proofed—Sec.								
13. Script Recorded—Coor.								
Recording Proofed—Prog.								
Recording Approved—SME								
14. Workbook Xeroxed—Sec.								
Criterion Test Xeroxed—Sec.								
15. Test Draft Compiled—Coor.								
16. Developmental Testing (date)								
17. Test Scored—SME, Prog.								
Test Results on Matrix—Prog.								
Test Analyzed—Prog.								
18. Test Conference—Coor.								
19. Revisions Complete—Prog.								
Revisions Edit—SME								
20. Workbook Revisions Retyped— Sec.								
Script Revisions Retyped—Sec.								
21. Script Recorded—Coor.								
Recording Checked—Prog.								
Workbook Xeroxed—Sec.								
22. Tape & Workbook Check—Coor.								
23. Prepare								
_____# Tapes_____								
_____# Workbooks _____								
_____# Tests _____								
24. Field Test (date)								
25. Test Scored—SME, Prog.								
Test Results on Matrix—Prog.								
Test Analyzed—Prog.								
26. Test Conference—Coor.								
27. Revisions Complete—Prog.								
Revisions Edit—SME								
28. Final Okay—Coor.								

mastery of the objectives. These two components are the basic aspects of the workbook in the Audio-Workbook instructional design. Correct answers (confirming feedback) to the questions will help to clarify the objectives—and the opposite is true as well.

Steps 6 through 14 are the stages for producing the audio instruction and compiling the workbook component. Since this is the stage at which the author will suggest a *different* approach to audio production, we will skip a description at this time until the entire Developmental Guide has been run through.

Steps 15 through 27 are developmental and field test validation procedures. Like any instructional program, the product which is being produced should be tested for its validity and reliability. Thus, the program should be tried out on students and pre- and post-tested for effectiveness. Where learning has not occurred, the program should be revised and tested again. Usually this can be done initially with a small group of students representative of the total student body of potential users—steps 15 through 18. Then, after initial revisions, it is tried on a larger group, usually in the actual field setting.

We shall now turn our attention to the production of the audio instruction itself.

Producing Audio on Its Own Terms

Written materials have always been produced (developed), quite naturally, from the written word. We sit down and write a manuscript. Audio as well, traditionally, has been produced *first* in the written word. A script is written and then recorded. Visuals have also traditionally been produced first in written form. The script is written and *then* visuals are added to accompany it. However, it would seem more logical to produce each of the media forms intially *on its own terms*. What does this mean?

Simply put, it means to begin development in the medium with which you are going to finish. In the same sense that we begin written programs in the written word, we should begin audio with audio, and visual with visual. Since we are concerned with audio here, this means beginning with a recording, rather than a written script. Why?

In general, we recognize that there are some differences in the written word and the spoken word. Written words often come out rather *stilted,* for example, when recorded. *Written words are not the way we necessarily talk, nor in the normal course of hearing, the way we usually hear.* The question to be answered, if possible, is whether the difference is important? But the answer is not that easy. It may depend on who is doing the talking and what they are talking about. It is important to realize, however, that we recognize that there is a need to equate the way we normally hear things with the way ideas are normally expressed. We might go so far as to say that it would be better for a student to produce the audio for other students because their means of *expression* is closer, most likely, than the generation which is producing the audio program.

Since we have in this particular instructional design both a written medium (the workbook) and an audio medium (the audio-tape), we can easily demonstrate how *producing each medium on its terms* can be accomplished. Indeed, the written medium will provide the direction for producing the audio medium. This procedure is illustrated step by step in Figure 6.

We begin by specifying the learning objectives. For both written and audio, in this instance, we need to know what the outcomes of instruction are to be; thus, the direction the production effort is to take. The author finds it most helpful, following the specification of objectives, to write

Figure 6

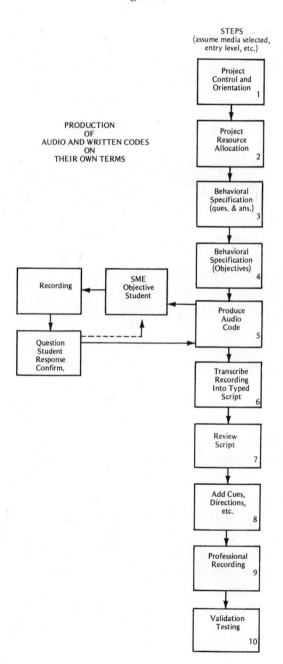

STEPS
(assume media selected,
entry level, etc.)

PRODUCTION
OF
AUDIO AND WRITTEN CODES
ON
THEIR OWN TERMS

Project Control and Orientation   1

Project Resource Allocation   2

Behavioral Specification (ques. & ans.)   3

Behavioral Specification (Objectives)   4

Recording

SME Objective Student

Produce Audio Code   5

Question Student Response Confirm.

Transcribe Recording Into Typed Script   6

Review Script   7

Add Cues, Directions, etc.   8

Professional Recording   9

Validation Testing   10

the questions (and answers) which will be used by students to test their mastery of the objectives. Writing the questions helps clarify the objectives. They also give more details than the relatively brief objective statements. Both the objectives and questions, which are the main elements of the workbook (the written medium), are then used to produce the audio instruction.

What the author recommends is that, if possible, three persons be brought together: the Instructional Designer, the Subject Matter Expert, and Student (or students).

If you are the designer and expert together, this is still satisfactory. The subject matter expert and the student sit down together, and the instructional designer observes. The subject matter expert hands the student, on a piece of paper, an objective or set of objectives. The student reads the objective, and then the subject matter expert turns on a cassette player, and proceeds to provide a verbal explanation of the objective. It is recommended that the subject matter expert be given a specific time limit within which to provide his explanation; otherwise, rambling is apt to occur. In this process, the student may ask questions or wait until after the verbal explanation is given. In any case, the student is ultimately asked to complete the question(s) which were written to check his mastery of the objective. Should the student be unable to perform satisfactorily, an exchange between subject matter expert and student would commence to determine the problem. This exchange is worth recording. *It is this recording*, then, that is used to develop the script. The recording is transcribed verbatim as a typed script and may, with due care, be reworked somewhat into a written script to be subsequently re-recorded. One must be careful in this process of reworking the script not to destroy many of the valuable *spoken forms of expression*. In some instances, the recording that is produced may be used as it comes out, or selected segments of it can be incorporated into the re-recorded tape.

A natural follow-through question to the above pro-cedure is: *Won't this procedure take me more time than if I just sat down and wrote out a script?* The answer is *Yes and No!* It does mean that you have to take the time to sit down with a student. Aside from this, an initial first-draft script is easier to produce in this manner because it is the time of a typist that is taken up in transcribing the recording to paper, rather than the writer's time. Even if it did take a little more time, there is the benefit of student feedback while you are *audio-writing*, so to speak. If you sit down to write a script, you would not have a student before you. Add this to the author's contention that producing a medium on its own terms is worthwhile, and you have benefits which make time of production seem insignificant within the total production effort.

VI.

RESOURCES

The following source material elaborates upon aspects of the Audio-Workbook design as described in this book:

BOOKS

Landgon, Danny G. *Interactive Instructional Designs for Individualized Learning.* Englewood Cliffs, N.J.: Educational Technology Publication, Inc., 1973.

Evans, Lionel and John Leedham. *Aspects of Educational Technology IX.* London, England: Kogan Page Limited, 1975.

ARTICLES

Langdon, Danny G., Media Messages on Their Own Terms. *Educational Technology*, June, 1972, pages 39-42.

Langdon, Danny G., Zimdex. *Training*, January, 1976, pages 26-27.

Rahmlow, Harold F., William Lewis and Danny G. Langdon. Audio Indexing for Individualization. *Audiovisual Instruction, 18*(4) April, 1973, pages 14-15.

IN USE AT

Several applications in the use of the Audio-Workbook are to be found in the programs offered by The American College, Bryn Mawr, Pennsylvania. Descriptive information about these programs may be obtained from The American College.

DANNY G. LANGDON is the Director of Instructional Design Research, The American College, Bryn Mawr, Pennsylvania. In his current capacity, Mr. Langdon conducts research to find more effective and efficient approaches to student learning. He has innovated several new approaches to learning, and is the founder of the Zimdex audio indexing system. Formerly a chemistry teacher in the U.S. Peace Corps and public, secondary education in the U.S.A., Mr. Langdon gained much of his experience in developing and researching instructional programs in education and business through his work at General Programmed Teaching, Inc., Palo Alto, California, and the Parks Job Corps Center, Pleasanton, California. Mr. Langdon has contributed several articles and a book, and has conducted workshops in the general field of Instructional Technology.